Original title:
A Love That Never Ends

Copyright © 2024 Creative Arts Management OÜ
All rights reserved.

Author: Philip Gomez
ISBN HARDBACK: 978-9916-94-836-1
ISBN PAPERBACK: 978-9916-94-837-8

Enduring Echoes

In the fridge, your leftovers stay,
They'll outlast us, come what may.
You snore like a bear, I still say cute,
Our dance in the kitchen? A muffin pursuit.

Your socks on the floor, a glorious sight,
I trip over them every night.
Yet, I wouldn't change a single thing,
Even if it makes my heart sing.

Eternal Mosaic

Your laughter echoes through the halls,
Like a racket from fourteen walls.
We bicker over which show to binge,
You'll always be my favorite cringe.

Every day brings a new silly fight,
Like who forgot to turn off the light.
Yet, when you smile, my heart sways,
In this painted chaos, I'll always stay.

Unbroken Dreams

We dreamt of riches, chips and cheese,
Instead, we got crumbs and sneezes.
Yet when you wink, the world's all right,
Even if we both can't see tonight.

You hold onto my arm in a twirl,
A spectacle, oh boy, what a whirl!
Life's a circus, and you're my clown,
With you, even melted ice cream won't frown.

Forever Yours

Your snarky comments keep me sane,
Who else would I blame in the rain?
We're a patchwork quilt of quirks and laughs,
With gnomes on our lawn making the halves.

Every morning, you snatch the best bite,
I pretend to scowl, but it feels so right.
Through all the chaos, grins and tears,
I'll choose you over all my fears.

Unfading Hearts

In a world of mismatched socks,
Our hearts beat to silly clocks.
You dance like a clumsy bear,
Yet I'm enchanted, unaware.

With toothpaste kisses on my cheek,
Your goofy laugh is all I seek.
We argue over what to eat,
Yet somehow, all this feels complete.

Endless Echoes of Affection

You snore like a runaway train,
But next to you, I'd brave the rain.
Our pillow talks are quite absurd,
Yet in your eyes, I see the world.

You steal my fries without a care,
But when you smile, I can't be bare.
With every quirk, my heart you win,
In this wild ride, let's begin.

Boundless Devotion

We play tag in the grocery lane,
Your shopping cart is not the same.
Together making quite the scene,
In our little love machine.

Your jokes are bad, but oh so sweet,
Like pineapple on pizza, a treat.
Through all the chaos, joy does bloom,
With you, my heart finds plenty of room.

The Infinite Dance

We tango with the garden hose,
In a dance that nobody knows.
You step on my toes, I start to laugh,
Our footprints make a silly path.

With laughter painted on our cheeks,
We navigate the daily leaks.
In every mess, there's joy we find,
A symphony of love, so blind.

Everlasting Promise

When I promised you my last french fry,
You burst into giggles, oh my oh my!
A vow so profound, yet it was quite sly,
But now you know, it's true love, not a lie.

We share odd socks and coffee spills,
In the midst of chaos, our heart still thrills.
With laughter and snacks, we conquer all hills,
Together we dance, where joy fulfills.

Boundless Affection

Your tickle fights leave me gasping for air,
While you giggle at my uncontrollable hair.
In a fairytale world, we'd make quite the pair,
Chasing each other with love, and some flair.

With midnight snacks fueled by our sweet delight,
We share silly secrets, staying up all night.
You steal the blanket, but it feels so right,
In your silly laughter, I find my light.

Timeless Threads

Embroidery threads can't measure our knits,
In this quilt of memories, every stitch fits.
Through tangled up yarn, our humor admits,
Together we weave, with giggles, not quits.

With tea and weird jokes, we spin off the charts,
Your punchlines engraving their place in my heart.
In our silly duet, all trouble departs,
Here's to many years—let's play our sweet parts.

Eternal Roses

You once tried to give me a rose made of cheese,
Saying, "I'm just being romantic, if you please!"
Your charm is infectious, it catches like bees,
In an endless bouquet of laughs and warm tease.

With garden gnomes watching, we burst into song,
Dancing like fools—we can do no wrong.
Through whimsical moments, our hearts stay strong,
In your quirky embrace, I gladly belong.

Forever Entangled

In socks that never match, we smile,
A dance of tangled laundry all the while.
With every twist and goofy glance,
We laugh as we do the laundry dance.

Forever tangled in our quirks,
You steal the cover while I smirk.
In bickering over who deserves the snack,
Our love's a comedy, that's a fact.

Unwavering Affection

You steal my fries, I take your cake,
In all the silly steps we make.
A shoe thrown here, a pillow fight,
In every jest, our hearts take flight.

Your snoring symphony serenades me,
While I plot my stealthy escape, you see.
Yet when you smile, I can't resist,
This unwavering bond is such a twist.

Endless Pathways

We stroll through life in clumsy shoes,
Falling for you still gives me the blues.
With paths so funny, we often trip,
But holding your hand makes my heart flip.

Every journey is an endless joke,
From losing keys to tripping on smoke.
With laughter echoing through each street,
In this crazy life, you're my favorite treat.

Ageless Connections

With inside jokes that never fade,
Our laughter's a timeless serenade.
From silly memes to playful jabs,
In our wild world, it's all a fab.

Through wrinkled skin, we still find grace,
In goofy faces, there's always space.
With age we might get a little bizarre,
But our joy together shines like a star.

The Unseen Thread

We share a bond with silly threads,
Like knitting with our feet instead.
Your laughter's like a perfect rhyme,
Knock-knock jokes that stand the time.

Together we dance on clumsy toes,
Chasing squirrels while everyone knows.
With every snort and cheeky grin,
Our crazy world will never thin.

When Stars Align Forever

Two dorks beneath the cosmic lights,
We plot the course of lunar flights.
Your milkshake brings the stars to play,
And cosmic giggles lead the way.

When planets crash and comets spin,
We stomp our feet to dance within.
Wobbly moves, we twirl and glide,
In this wild ride, I'm on your side.

Evermore in Bloom

Our garden's filled with flowers bright,
Though some are weeds that grow with might.
You pick the blooms, and I pick fights,
With pollen allergies on our nights.

In pots of laughter, joy will sprout,
With every daft joke without a doubt.
Through April showers and sunny rays,
We bask in blooms on silly days.

Shadows of Forever

In shadows cast from moonlit beams,
We share our dreams and ice cream themes.
Your elbow's sharp; it's quite absurd,
Yet those are moments fondly heard.

We dance in puddles, skipping stones,
Laughing loudly, breaking bones.
Every mishap, every little fall,
Declares our bond, the silliest of all.

Endless Serenade

In a world of mismatched socks,
We dance to the sound of clocks.
Your laugh—a melody so sweet,
In my heart, you have a seat.

We tickle fate with silly glee,
You're the jelly to my bee.
Through clumsy falls and awkward sights,
We serenade our silly nights.

Unfading Joy

Like pizza topped with extra cheese,
Your grin can melt my worries with ease.
We joke about our growing hair,
And laugh like we haven't a care.

With your quirks, you light my way,
Like bright socks on a sunny day.
In this silly game we play,
Joy is here, and it's here to stay.

Timeless Heartbeat

Your snore is music, can't you see?
Like a classic tune on repeat.
With every sigh and goofy grin,
My heart races—let the fun begin.

We're like two peas in a pod,
You with your chance of odd.
Each day is like a brand-new song,
In our playful world, we belong.

An Endless Journey

We travel roads that twist and turn,
But with you, I've much to learn.
From road trips filled with snacks galore,
To detours that leave us wanting more.

With signs that say, 'No U-Turns please,'
We laugh and munch on stale cheese.
In the map of life, you're my guide,
In this joyride, I take pride.

Constant Companionship

You stole my fries, it's true,
But I still share my ice cream too.
A sock on the floor, that's your style,
Together we laugh, it's always worthwhile.

From silly dances to goofy pranks,
We've built a bond, no need for thanks.
Two peas in a pod, totally absurd,
Companions for life, haven't you heard?

Perpetual Heartbeat

My heartbeat skips, when you snore,
Yet I'd never trade this, not for more.
You're the ketchup to my fries,
The twinkle in my sleepy eyes.

In the chaos of life, you bring delight,
Even when you argue, morning and night.
A dance in the kitchen, oh what a sight,
With you, everything feels just right!

Timeless Reflections

In the mirror's gaze, we both see,
A couple of goofballs, you and me.
Our selfies are wild, hair askew,
But together, we've made quite a view.

We'll rock the world in our own way,
With mismatched socks, come what may.
In laughter and fun, we'll always dwell,
Caught in our bubble, it's simply swell!

Infinite Emotions

You make me smile in ways so absurd,
Like when you talk to our pet bird.
With endless jokes and playful jests,
Who knew love could be one big fest?

Through all the quirks, we always find,
A way to be silly, sweet, and kind.
With every tickle, and playful tease,
Together we're cozy, like warm summer breeze.

Limitless Devotion

Your socks are never matched, that's true,
But my heart will always wear your hue.
You steal the covers every night,
Yet, I can't help but find it quite alright.

We trip over shoes just to dance,
Laughing together at our goofy stance.
With every spilled drink, love's a new game,
Your silly antics, they never bring shame.

When you snore like a truck in a dream,
I'll bring you coffee, you know what I mean.
My heart's a plot twist, it makes me grin,
In the sitcom of life, you're my favorite win.

Perpetual Connection

I'll wear your t-shirt, it's oversized,
In the sunshine, how you get mesmerized.
Through kitchen disasters and burnt toast,
Your laughter is what I love the most.

You keep the remote, it's a fact I know,
But I smile as you hog it like a pro.
With popcorn fights and movie nights,
It's like I'm flying on love's wild flights.

When the dog steals my food off the plate,
You grab it back and say, 'Ain't that great?'
Every little mess, every silly brawl,
Our quirky love conquers it all.

Unfading Radiance

You steal my fries and I let you,
Because your grin is my favorite view.
You dance in the rain with a silly hat,
Making a splash, how about that?

Waking you up is a daily delight,
With your bedhead, you give such a fright!
Your jokes are so corny, they make me roll,
Yet each punchline gets me, heart and soul.

As wrinkles appear, it's still the same,
With belly laughs, I call your name.
In this comedy, we take our part,
With every chuckle, you capture my heart.

Ageless Yearning

We bicker for hours on the silliest things,
Like who gets the last bite and who sings.
Our secret code needs a dictionary,
Yet in our chaos, we find the merry.

The calendar's marked with dates we keep,
Like movie marathons that never sleep.
With ice cream for dinner, we craft our day,
In our playful world, we never sway.

When you forget where you put your keys,
It's hard to stay mad when you smile with ease.
In every mishap, from start to end,
You'll always be my forever friend.

Timeless Affection

In a world of giggles and cheer,
We dance like no one's near.
Your socks don't match, but that's just fine,
I'll love your quirks, as you'll love mine.

With every joke and pun we share,
Your goofy grin is quite the snare.
Together we're a silly pair,
In laughter's grip, we'll always care.

Endless Embrace

We hug like we're stuck in a door,
It's awkward, but oh, I want more.
Your clumsy charm lights up the day,
In your arms, I want to stay.

With dance moves that defy all grace,
We twirl around, a silly race.
Though we may fall, it's never tough,
Your laugh just says, 'That's quite enough!'

Infinite Heartstrings

Your heart plays like a rusty lute,
Yet every note's a sweet pursuit.
With jingles from our quirky jokes,
We'll serenade the happy folks.

In this symphony of silliness,
Your funny face, I can't suppress.
Strummed together, we sing our song,
In notes of joy, where we belong.

Forever Entwined

We're wrapped up tight, like two old vines,
Tangled up in silly times.
Your socks are bold, your hair's a mess,
But I can't help but love you best.

Through mishaps and our silly fights,
You steal the covers almost every night.
Yet here we are, two peas in a pod,
In laughter's glow, we're blessed, not flawed.

Unending Tide

You stole my fries, I stole your heart,
A friendship forged with a sneaky start.
We laugh at jokes that make no sense,
In our goofy world, there's no recompense.

The ocean rolls, but so does our wit,
Like two silly seals, we just can't quit.
With tidal waves of laughter so grand,
In this funny dance, we hand in hand.

From sunup surprises to late-night pranks,
With every splash, we fill in the blanks.
You keep me rolling, and I keep you sane,
In the currents of joy, we'll never refrain.

So here we float, on this sea of cheer,
With every giggle, I hold you near.
Our silly saga, a whimsical ride,
Forever afloat on this unending tide.

Where Hearts Align

In a coffee shop, we brewed a plan,
I spilled my drink, you laughed — oh man!
With every stumble, our rhythm grows,
Like two left feet in a dance on toes.

We share inside jokes, a wild delight,
And argue 'bout pizza toppings at night.
With pineapple madness, we don't agree,
But together we make the best kind of spree.

The stars may twinkle, the moon gives a wink,
We share all our secrets quicker than you think.
In fumbles and giggles, our hearts beat fast,
In this quirky union, I've found my cast.

So here's to our journey, delightfully bright,
Where laughter and chaos merge day and night.
When the world feels heavy, we'll take off and fly,
In the cosmos above, where our hearts align.

Evermore Enchantment

You cast a spell with that charming grin,
With each little chuckle, let the fun begin!
A wand of laughter, a potion of glee,
In our own fairy tale, just you and me.

From magic tricks to silly rhymes,
We dodge the clock, ignore the times.
With playful banter, we'll paint the skies,
In our whimsical world, all worries minimize.

You're the wizard, and I'm your muse,
In the land of nonsense, we cannot lose.
With wings of a fairy, we dance through the air,
Casting enchantments beyond compare.

So let's spin around in this wondrous trance,
With sprinkles of laughter, we're ready to prance.
In a realm where giggles endlessly soar,
You and I, forever, in evermore.

Nonstop Serenade

You serenade me with your silly song,
A rhythm so catchy, I just can't go wrong.
With every chorus, my heart starts to dance,
In this nonstop tune, we take our chance.

We strum on our dreams with mismatched chords,
While stealing the show with our goofy rewards.
Your voice makes me giggle, your style makes me sway,
In this joyful duet, we brighten the gray.

With harmonies sweet like a candy delight,
You tickle my fancy, oh what a sight!
Side by side, we'll conquer the stage,
In a comedy act, we'll center the rage.

So here's to our song, forever we'll play,
In a world full of laughter, it's where we'll stay.
In this endless serenade, we'll never fade,
For you are my music, my heart's masquerade.

Eternal Embrace

In the fridge, your snacks are stored,
I found your socks, now they're adored.
You stole the blanket, such a fuss,
Yet here I am, still loving us.

Your snoring sounds like a cat in fright,
But I'll keep you close every night.
In every quarrel, we make a scene,
Yet, here we dance like we're still teens.

Your quirky laugh brightens my day,
Who knew love could be such a play?
You make me giggle, you make me sigh,
With every joke, we can't deny.

Through silly fights and playful grins,
Our secret's out, let the laughter begin.
In all our quirks, we find our fate,
Embracing this chaos, isn't it great?

Timeless Whispers

You call me names like 'Snugglebug',
Yet you still give me a warm hug.
In our own world, where laughter reigns,
We're reading maps to wacky terrains.

You stole my fries, you rascal, you,
But what's a meal without a feud?
We share our dreams of fancy cars,
Yet giggle at our set of jars.

With whispers sweet and cereal spills,
I cherish you through all the thrills.
Every hiccup, every laugh line,
Binds us closer, your heart's divine.

In the twilight, we dance on air,
With mismatched socks and unkempt hair.
A mismatched puzzle, we fit just fine,
With each playful jab, your heart is mine.

Forever Entwined

Two left feet on the dance floor,
But we laugh hard, who needs more?
Your weird quirks, like singing loud,
Make me proud, oh look at us now.

Your cooking burns but my heart's aflame,
Each charred bite adds to our game.
We make a mess, it's our own art,
Even the chaos plays a part.

With secret jokes and playful shoves,
In this tangle, we find our loves.
You read my mind, or do I yours?
In frames of laughter, our heart tours.

In every laugh, in every sigh,
Our love's a joke, we can't deny.
Entwined we stand, like vines so bold,
Forever wrapped, our tales unfold.

Infinities of Us

You say I steal the covers, what a lie!
I'm just testing if you can fly.
In this circus called life, we run wild,
With goofy grins just like a child.

Our love is quirky, a playful tease,
With endless puns that put us at ease.
We're mismatched socks, but that's our style,
I wouldn't trade you, not for a mile.

Through rolling eyes and silly fights,
We spin together like starlit nights.
In every glance, I find a reason,
To celebrate you in every season.

You're my partner in this hilarious race,
With knack for making even frowns face.
Infinities of chuckles, I can't resist,
Together forever, sealed with a twist.

Constant Canvas

Your smile is like a work of art,
I paint it daily, not a dark part.
With every laugh and silly dance,
We're two Bob Rosses in a trance.

Our love's a canvas, splashes bright,
With mismatched socks, a fanciful sight.
Every quirk and silly feat,
Make this masterpiece complete.

Eternal Whispers

In whispers soft like bubbling brew,
We share the secrets, just us two.
You snore a tune, I giggle loud,
Our midnight chats draw quite a crowd.

Like socks that vanish in the wash,
Our silly tales make me want to posh.
Forever friends, we play and jest,
In this comic book, we're the best!

Infinite Horizon

Together we gaze at skies so wide,
Chasing clouds as they decide.
Your jokes are corny, but I don't mind,
In your laughter, joy I find.

We'll roam the streets with whimsical glee,
Finding treasures under every tree.
With you, every day is bright and new,
Like a wanderlust with a silly view.

Boundless Time

In the clock of life, you're my tick-tock,
Silly songs at every block.
We dance with time, all quirky steps,
Collecting laughter, perhaps some mishaps.

Every moment with you is pure delight,
Like finding snacks at midnight.
In this race, we take our time,
With laughter as our favorite rhyme.

Unbroken Ties

In the garden of quirks we bloom,
With laughter that chases away gloom.
You steal my fries, I steal your drink,
Together we're chaos, yet we still sync.

We dance to a tune only we know,
Your silly jokes always steal the show.
Like mismatched socks, we make quite a pair,
With you by my side, I've not a care.

Through ticklish moments and silly fights,
We find our way back to cozy nights.
Like two goofy peas in a funky pod,
Our bond is so silly, it's truly odd.

Forever united in playful spree,
Even your snoring means love to me.
With goofy grins and playful sighs,
Our hearts are forever, that's no surprise.

Ageless Longing

Like fine wine, we age in jest,
With endless stories, we're truly blessed.
You mock my hair and I pout in play,
Yet in every laugh, I long to stay.

Your quirky laugh is my daily dose,
In a world of vanilla, you're rich like rose.
Counting the days till our next silly fight,
Even then I'll find you, my heart's delight.

In a circus of love, I'm the clown,
You paint my gray days with a frown.
Through wacky dances and rhyming meals,
The joy that you bring is all that one feels.

So here we stand, hand in hand,
In a dance of awkward, we make our stand.
Even with pranks that spark and ignite,
Together we shine, oh what a sight!

Beyond the Horizon of Hearts

Our friendship's a ship with sails of dreams,
Drifting on waters of laughter and beams.
With jokes that land like quirky arrows,
We shoot for the stars while giggling in meadows.

In this vast ocean of whimsical delight,
We navigate storms with a heartwarming fight.
Your puns are the compass that guides my way,
In this silly voyage, I'd forever stay.

With treasures found in the depths of each joke,
We breathe in the sand, feel the sun we evoke.
From punchlines to hugs, our routine's a thrill,
Past the horizon, we dance at will.

No waves can drown this buoyant cheer,
In our world of chuckles, all feels so clear.
Across every distance, every hearty jest,
I cherish each moment; you're simply the best.

Everlasting Bonds

In a land of giggles, our hearts reside,
Where each silly moment is our joyride.
You prank me twice, then I prank you back,
Oh, the laughter in this colorful track.

With rubber chickens and dancing shoes,
We march through life, breaking all news.
Our silly debates on who loves more,
Lead to ice cream battles, and that's for sure!

From playful nudges to ticklish blows,
In raucous laughter, true love shows.
Even in chaos, we thrive and play,
Together forever, come what may.

Through thick and thin, we'll laugh till we share,
The wittiest memories beyond compare.
With every tease, my heart pings a song,
In this funny adventure, we both belong.

Unyielding Journey

We walked together, side by side,
You with your snacks, me with my pride.
In puddles we jumped, and slipped with glee,
Who knew, dear partner, just you and me?

Through forests and fields, our laughter rings,
Like two clumsy penguins with flapping wings.
We may bicker over which show to binge,
But I'd never trade you, not for an orange fringe!

The road stretches on, it twists and it bends,
You're the comedy act that never descends.
With each silly moment, my heart gets a boost,
Together we giggle, a joyful noose!

To a future unknown, we both set our sights,
Where every odd quirk just feels so right.
Through thick and through thin, we're here to stay,
Chasing sunsets and cake, come what may!

Eternal Symmetry

You steal the covers, I claim the bed,
The perfect equation, our laughter widespread.
In the kitchen, we dance, no rhythm in sight,
With flour in our hair, we still feel alright.

Your puns are relentless, a true heartfelt crime,
But my eye-rolling laughter is quite sublime.
We share cheesy jokes, and a block of cheese,
Our love is a riddle, wrapped up with ease.

Through ups and through downs, we wobble and sway,
Like clowns on a trampoline, that's our way!
When life throws us lemons, we make lemon meringue,
In this wacky duet, our hearts are the gang.

So here's to the madness, the giggles we share,
With you as my partner, life's a circus affair.
We may never grow up, always play the fool,
In this perfect symmetry, you're my golden rule!

Ageless Love Songs

In mismatched pajamas, we sing off-key,
Our voices a melody, insane but free.
With popcorn confetti, we dance in our chair,
Finding pure bliss in the chaos we share.

At midnight we plot, how to conquer the fridge,
With pickle juice revels, we leap like a bridge.
You navigate maps while I eat your fries,
Together we laugh till we tear up our eyes.

The playlist of life is a funny duet,
Each tune tells a tale that we won't regret.
With you as my muse, each verse always bright,
In this song of affection, all wrongs feel so right.

As years march along, we'll join in the fun,
With wigs and with crutches when we're overrun.
In this ageless tale, we won't miss a beat,
For our love is the rhythm that makes us complete!

Endless Horizons

With each sunrise, I find you awake,
Sketching the world while I'm still half-baked.
You tickle my brain with a wild idea,
Let's fly with the seagulls, or at least have a beer!

In the park we chase squirrels, and trip on the grass,
You say it's the fun that makes time go fast.
Our plans are a jumble, a beautiful mess,
Like socks on a line, we just can't confess.

When the stars light the sky, we count to a hundred,
In puddles of laughter, our hearts feel unblended.
We juggle the moments, like fruit in the air,
With you by my side, there's no room for despair.

So here's to the journey, let's give it a go,
With shenanigans waiting and hours to throw.
In this grand escapade, my friend, my delight,
Our endless horizons feel perfectly bright!

Beyond the Sands of Time

We dance on grains, with silly grins,
Each moment tickles, as laughter wins.
Time's silly clock, it turns around,
In our goofy love, joy is found.

With every tick, we bump and fall,
I trip on words, you wink through it all.
Sands fly by, yet here we stand,
In chuckles shared, hand in hand.

Mismatched socks and playful fights,
We turn the darkness into lights.
Time may blur, but not our cheer,
In every laugh, you're always near.

So here we spin, no cares to bind,
Our goofy hearts, forever intertwined.
Through grains of sand, let laughter chime,
As we play on, beyond all time.

An Unwritten Forever

Our story's blank, yet ink will flow,
With doodles bright, our hearts will glow.
Page by page, we sketch and glee,
In this wild tale, it's you and me.

Coffee spills, and stray cat naps,
Frogs in tuxedos, and silly traps.
Unwritten lines where laughter sprouts,
Our funny quest, no doubts about.

Jellybean dreams and rubber ducks,
We conjure smiles with little luck.
Adventures bloom like flowers in spring,
In this unwritten, we'll weave our zing.

So scribble on, with joyous pen,
This playful story will never end.
With every twist, a giggle's call,
In this empty book, we'll write it all.

The Unyielding Flame

In flickering light, our chuckles soar,
You set my heart ablaze, for sure.
A candle's dance, we laugh so loud,
In this warm glow, we're love's proud crowd.

The pizza burns, we burst with glee,
Flaming marshmallows, just you and me.
With silly sparks, the night ignites,
We roast our dreams on starry nights.

Witty banter, like fireflies fly,
In our bright flame, no need to shy.
As long as we keep the laughter near,
This dancing fire will never fear.

So let it blaze, our joyful spark,
As giggles glow within the dark.
In all we've claimed, we will remain,
A funny tale, our unyielding flame.

Embracing Infinity

We loop and twirl like silly loops,
In this embrace, we make our goofs.
Infinity, a giant hug,
With laughter wrapped, all snug as a bug.

Time might stretch, like rubber bands,
We draw our dreams in wiggly sands.
Riding waves of giggles bright,
In our funny dance, we take flight.

Every cheeky quirk, a playful kiss,
In our wacky world, there's endless bliss.
So here we are, like twinkling stars,
In this dance of joy, we'll go far.

With every loop, we twirl and sway,
Embracing laughs along the way.
So take my hand, don't let it slip,
In this infinity, we'll freely skip.

The Bind of Infinity

In the kitchen, we dance, a quirky two,
You steal my fries, and I chase you too.
With every giggle, the clock slows down,
In this silly circus, we wear the crown.

Your socks don't match, but I find it grand,
We tackle life with a spaghetti strand.
Every blunder, a stitch in our quilt,
In this laughter-filled world, our hearts are built.

Side by side, we face the day,
Through spilled coffee and funny cliché,
Our bathroom selfies, a masterpiece,
With each silly pose, our joy will increase.

So here's to us, forever a pair,
In this jumbled love, we never despair.
Hand in hand, we embark with glee,
In the bind of forever, just you and me.

A Symphony of Timelessness

Your tunes are off, yet I sing along,
With pots and pans, we create our song.
Swinging the broom, you miss my toe,
In this goofy duet, we steal the show.

Each laugh's a note, in our endless score,
Though you can't dance, I love you more.
With flatulent sounds that echo the night,
Our harmonies clash but never lose sight.

We age like cheese, a bit strong at best,
But our happy chaos beats all the rest.
With pranks and chuckles, we'll never grow old,
In this symphonic life, our hearts are bold.

So let's raise a cup to our wild, sweet tune,
Understated magic beneath the moon.
In this timeless jest, let's spin and sway,
With laughter and love, we'll dance every day.

Ever Present, Ever True

Your antics are wild, like a cat on a wall,
When you trip on your laces, you laugh, I fall.
With silly remarks that never grow tired,
In moments like these, our hearts are inspired.

The hiccups you get when you sip too fast,
Results in giggles that will always last.
With every blunder, I see the light,
In this carnival ride, our future is bright.

You hide my keys, I savor the chase,
Even after all these years, it's still a race.
We share our secrets in whispers of glee,
Every day with you is pure jubilee.

So here's to us, forever in jest,
Picking each other, we both are blessed.
In the chapters we write, it's all so true,
Ever present joy, just me and you.

Chapters of a Boundless Tale

In the library, we create a fuss,
Reaching for books, I accidentally push.
With laughter echoing off every wall,
We write our story, daring and tall.

Your quirky bookmarks are just a mess,
With doodles and sketches that confess.
Every page turned, a smile unfolds,
In our boundless tale, adventure holds.

We fight over popcorn during every show,
Your side is salty; mine's a sweet flow.
While movies roll, our commentary flies,
In our own screenplay, laughter never dies.

So let's pen our saga, a crazy delight,
Through mishaps and laughter, days and nights.
With you at my side, let's set sail and bail,
In this wild journey, our boundless tale.

Immortal Touch

In an old, cozy chair, we sit with a grin,
Eating popcorn, while bickering begins.
You steal my fries, then I take your drink,
This love's like fine cheese, it only does stink.

Laughing and teasing, we dance in the rain,
Your socks are now soggy, but who feels the pain?
We're stuck like two books on a shelf side by side,
If love is a journey, we just took a ride.

Unyielding Adoration

With your endless antics, you keep me on toes,
One day a taco, the next, a pink hose.
Your puns are my treasure, I delve through each joke,
Like a quirky old dog, you never will choke.

A serenade sung in the off-keyest way,
You make me burst out with laughter each day.
In silly old pajamas, we'll dance till we drop,
This wacky connection? It just won't stop.

Timeless Souls

In a world that's spinning, we giggle and tease,
Like two silly squirrels who just discovered some cheese.
With your funny faces, I can't help but grin,
We'll laugh 'til the end, let the good times begin.

The clock ticks away, but we don't seem to care,
Your sock puppet jokes give life a fresh air.
Through quirks and the chaos, we juggle our dreams,
Two timeless old souls, bursting at the seams.

Infinite Togetherness

With laughter like echoes, we float through the days,
Hosting wild parties in a million odd ways.
You trip on your shoelace, I spill my hot tea,
Yet somehow, it feels like pure harmony.

In matching sweaters, we make quite the scene,
Like clowns in a circus, so silly and keen.
Forever's our mantra, but let's keep it light,
Together we shine, like stars in the night.

Transcendent Union

In a world of mismatched socks,
We dance with twinkling clocks.
Your laugh, a bubble, bright and bold,
Keeps me warm when nights are cold.

We argue over pizza toppings,
Yet find joy in all our floppings.
With every pun and silly tease,
Our hearts find ways to just say cheese.

Through all the silly, crazy fights,
You steal the covers every night.
But when the sun begins to rise,
It's you that always wins the prize.

So let's keep dancing through our days,
In our delightfully silly ways.
Together, we can face the trends,
With a bond that never bends.

Ceaseless Melody

Your voice, a tune that grips my heart,
Like singing cats in the park.
We harmonize in quirky rhyme,
Creating songs that stop all time.

Every note, a joyful shout,
You bring the beats, I'll bring the clout.
With laughter as our common thread,
We make symphonies in our bed.

Through ups and downs, in jests we glide,
Your smirk, my favorite joyride.
In the chorus of our silly fights,
Our love shines brighter than city lights.

So here's my heart, wrapped in a song,
Where every foolish moment belongs.
In this dance, we're far from apart,
With melodies that fill the heart.

Infinite Moments

In our garden of endless pranks,
We whistle at the way life wanks.
With butterflies that giggle and tease,
Each moment blooms like springtime bees.

We chase the clouds on rainy days,
Muddy puddles, goofy displays.
With every splash and silly grin,
We remind the world that love can win.

From cooking fails to burnt delights,
We dine on laughter, sipping Heights.
In the kitchen, chaos may reign,
But sweeter stories linger like rain.

So here's to moments, wild and free,
With you, it's pure insanity.
Together we craft this merry blend,
In antics that will never end.

Immortal Wishes

If wishes were ticklish stars,
We'd ride on cosmic candy cars.
Through futures that we whimsically spin,
Hand in hand, forever we win.

Prancing 'round with quirky dreams,
You make me laugh until it seams.
In the book of life, we scribble clear,
Each page is filled with love and cheer.

As clocks go dizzy with our pace,
Time trips over in this race.
With every wink and clumsy fall,
Our hearts invent the silliest call.

Let's blow the candles on absurdity,
With wishes wrapped in certainty.
In the garden of playful flair,
Our joyous laughter fills the air.

Timeless Tryst

In socks that clash, we laugh out loud,
Your dance moves clear the bustling crowd.
With each spilled drink, we share a grin,
Our timeless tryst, where sparks begin.

The cat disapproves, gives us a stare,
Yet we keep twirling without a care.
With pillows as shields in our silly fight,
This goofy love feels just so right.

We trip on shoes left in the hall,
Your silly jokes, they make me fall.
In every mishap, a giggle's born,
Our hearts, together, forever sworn.

We snicker under the moonlit sky,
With stars as witnesses as we sigh.
In this joyful mess, you are my friend,
Together we'll laugh, our rules we bend.

Unfaltering Passion

We argue 'bout the movie choice,
Yet in your eyes, I hear your voice.
With popcorn kernels stuck in your hair,
This unfaltering passion fills the air.

We share a sandwich, one half each,
And fight for bites, that's how we teach.
In every moment, you make me smile,
Together we'll laugh, mile after mile.

Your cooking skills? A bit of a joke,
But when you laugh, my heart's sure woke.
From burnt toast mornings to midnight snacks,
I chase your giggles, ignore the cracks.

In awkward dances, we spin around,
With two left feet, we're glory bound.
Through every quirk and silly stunt,
Our love's a funny, joyous hunt.

Relentless Tenderness

You stole my fries, but that's alright,
For every bite shared feels so light.
With ketchup smudged on your cheek so bright,
This relentless tenderness feels just right.

Our silly selfies, faces all goofy,
No filter needed, life's so loopy.
In every moment, joy's our creed,
We plant pure laughter, love is the seed.

Your snoring like a bear, it's quite a scene,
But in my heart, you reign as queen.
Through raucous nights and morning gripes,
This loving bond turns quips into types.

In car karaoke, we sing out loud,
With off-key notes, we stand so proud.
With every chuckle, our hearts extend,
In this joyous dance, we shall not end.

Forever in Bloom

With flowers that wilt from our wild play,
You twirl around, I'm lost in your sway.
Your quirky hats make me chuckle loud,
In this garden of laughter, we're forever proud.

We plant our dreams in silly pots,
With watering cans, we forget the thoughts.
In this colorful chaos, giggles abide,
With every bloom, we let love slide.

The bees dance close, they want to know,
How we create our glowy show.
In petal fights and garden strolls,
Your laughter fills my heart and souls.

In every season, the jokes grow strong,
With you by my side, where I belong.
This joyful journey, hand in hand,
Forever in bloom, we make our stand.

Infinite Quietude

In the silence, we still scream,
Your snoring's part of my dream.
Together we sit, eat some pie,
While our cat gives us a sly eye.

In our world, time takes a break,
Life's too short for any heartache.
You juggle socks, I giggle loud,
Annoyed blissful, we stand proud.

Tickle fights at the break of dawn,
You steal the covers, then I yawn.
Coffee spills, we laugh and cheer,
Your silly dance brings me good cheer.

Our love's a circus, wild and bright,
With popcorn dreams and sheer delight.
Hand in hand, we take a bow,
In this act of madness, I love you now.

Perennial Joy

You stole my fries, but that's okay,
I guess I love you more each day.
Your silly puns, oh what a thrill,
Make my heart dance against its will.

In a world of socks that don't match,
We find sweet joy, like making a catch.
Your goofy grin, it lights my way,
In this wild ride, I want to stay.

We share bad jokes, the kind that stick,
While you try hard to do magic tricks.
Every mishap turns into a spree,
How could life be better, just you and me?

Together we laugh under the stars,
Counting wishes on candy bars.
In our game of silly, let me say,
With you forever, I'll always stay.

Everlasting Sunrise

Each morning brings your coffee song,
With every sip, you can't go wrong.
The sun may rise, but not as bright,
As your silly face at morning light.

Pajama days become our norm,
In cozy chaos, we find our form.
A pillow fight by noon's embrace,
Laughing hard, it's our happy place.

In seasonal giggles that never fade,
You try to dance; I'm too afraid.
But with every twirl, I can't help but grin,
In this silly game, I'll never give in.

Our hearts beat in a quirky song,
A rhythm that can't be wrong.
With you near, the world feels bright,
Together creating our own daylight.

Limitless Vows

You and I, we've made a mess,
With our laundry pile, I must confess.
Yet every sock tells our tale,
Of adventures grand and epic fails.

In sweater forts, we hide away,
Making plans for our perfect day.
Your silly hat just makes me laugh,
We dance in circles, no need for a path.

Love notes written in crayon bold,
Silly stickers, emotions sold.
Each day with you is a fresh parade,
In the chaos of life, our dreams won't fade.

Our vows are jokes, but they hold true,
In giggles and grins, it's just me and you.
As we grow old, I'll still be your fan,
For this endless ride, let's make our plan.

In the Garden of Endless Affection

In the garden where you tripped,
You've planted all your jokes and quips.
The daisies laugh, they can't be shy,
While butterflies swoop in to pry.

Your puns sprout like weeds in cheer,
While I giggle, holding back a tear.
The sunbeams dance upon our heads,
As love blooms brightly in flower beds.

We pick tomatoes, squish 'em tight,
And laugh as they moonwalk in their plight.
A squirrel steals crumbs from our plate,
While we giggle at our own fate.

So in this garden, wild and bright,
Our raucous laughter takes to flight.
Together we sow joy and jest,
In this patch, we feel so blessed.

The Canvas of Our Forever.

With splashes of color, we start to paint,
A canvas filled with jokes so quaint.
Your brush slips, and blue spills wide,
But I just laugh, my arms open wide.

Every stroke is a shared little quirk,
You paint a cat and give it a smirk.
I splash red just to draw your ire,
Creating a chaos that never tires.

In colors bright, our laughter mingles,
With every mishap, a new tale jangles.
A masterpiece born of whimsy's might,
In our gallery, love stays in sight.

As we stand back, it's a vibrant mess,
Yet our hearts sing in sheer happiness.
Forever's canvas, oh what a charm,
In each silly stroke, we're safe from harm.

Eternal Echoes

In the hallway of our funny past,
Echoes of laughter, forever cast.
You dropped the cake, it made a splat,
And now each slice sits with a hat!

Through every giggle, a cherished sound,
My heart chuckles, love knows no bound.
We reminisce with snacks in hand,
While the echoes of silliness grand.

Our memories dancing, wild and free,
In the chambers of this heart's decree.
You tease my jokes, adoringly so,
It's a banter fest, don't steal the show!

Past the doors, love's sweet refrain,
Echoes of joy, like a playful gain.
In every giggle, our hearts converse,
In this timeless tale, we immerse.

Boundless Whispers

In secret corners, our whispers play,
Like mischievous sprites leading the way.
You mutter silliness beneath the stars,
While I giggle, imagining Mars.

Through ticklish secrets we silently share,
You make me laugh without a care.
A gentle nudge, a joking tease,
In our world, we do as we please.

Each soft whisper, a humorous jest,
Keeping our hearts joyfully blessed.
No moonlight's needed, just our bright smiles,
As laughter carries us over the miles.

In boundless whispers, forever we bask,
Twirling in moments that ask and ask.
With every jest, our spirits soar,
Together forever, who could want more?

Ceaseless Dreams

In a land where socks go missing,
We dance on crumbs, not kissing.
Your snore's a serenade at night,
With every breach, we laugh, take flight.

We share the quirkiest of schemes,
Like planting flowers in our dreams.
Your laughter's like a lively tune,
When you steal my fries, I swoon!

Oh, how your jokes can crack a grin,
Even when our plans wear thin.
Through every blunder, we both strive,
Together forever, oh what a jive!

With tangled sheets and silly fights,
You make my days feel oh so bright.
In every whimsy, silly act,
Our hearts remain forever intact.

Unbroken Bonds

You hide my keys, I tease your hair,
In every glance, there's love to share.
We binge on shows, our snacks combine,
With every laugh, fate draws the line.

We'll dance like dorks in grocery stores,
Then chase our cat, beneath the doors.
Your puns, like bubbles, never burst,
In our sweet chaos, we've both rehearsed.

When pizza's gone, we hit the floor,
Who knew we'd need to fight for more?
In cooking fails, we spark delight,
Together in this endless night.

Our bonds grow strong with silly drills,
Like looking for lost rainbow pills.
With every twist, this tale we weave,
In laughter's grip, we still believe.

Everlasting Flame

In the kitchen, you light a fire,
While I just try to dodge your ire.
We burn the toast but laugh instead,
Your giggle's like a warm bedspread.

Your wild ideas, oh where to start?
From crazy games to midnight art.
We paint the walls in colors bright,
With every splash, there's pure delight.

When life gets tough, we play pretend,
As superheroes, we won't bend.
With capes and masks, we hit the street,
Together, oh, what an epic feat!

Through silly fights and goofy trends,
In every tale, our fun transcends.
As long as we have laughs to claim,
Our hearts will blaze like an endless flame.

Eternal Dance

We shimmy through the living room,
With socks that glide, we chase the gloom.
Your finicky feet step on my toes,
Yet in this dance, our laughter grows.

With every spin, the dog joins in,
A trio of chaos, we all grin.
We twirl through days of socks and shoes,
In our fun world, we'll never lose.

Your wiggly moves, a sight to see,
In every misstep, you're still with me.
As kitchen dishes do their song,
In our forever, where we belong.

So here we are, a pair of fools,
Defying all the dancing rules.
With every laugh, our spirits prance,
In the endless rhythm of our dance.

Whispers through Eternity

In the garden, we dance and twirl,
With mismatched socks, oh what a whirl!
Your laugh is a song, a joyful tease,
Like butterflies tickling the summer breeze.

Each morning you steal my last slice of toast,
Then claim that my snoring is what you hate most.
But with each silly bicker and playful fight,
I can't help but grin, you make my heart light.

We share old dreams like we share our clothes,
With polka dots tonight, who knows how it goes?
You weave funny tales that leave me in stitches,
Our love's a jigsaw with silly glitches.

So let's raise a glass to our quirky affair,
With your goofy dance moves and wild, frizzy hair.
In this hilarious world, we'll forever glide,
With laughter as fuel, we'll take life in stride.

The Heart's Infinite Journey

Your texts make me giggle, I can't deny,
Like that time I sent you a winky pie.
You reply with memes that make no sense,
Yet somehow you charm with your nonsense pretense.

Through trials of time, we bumble and blunder,
You hide the remote; it puts me in thunder!
Yet every mishap, oh, what a delight,
We'll laugh through the bumps—dance through the night.

I'll whisk you away in my messy old car,
With snacks on the floor and the radio bizarre.
Each laugh we share is a map, oh so fine,
Tracing paths of the love that's uniquely divine.

So let's wander together, just you and I,
With mismatched shoes and dreams that fly high.
We'll giggle our way over valleys and hills,
With jokes that burst forth like love's endless thrills.

Threads of Time and Tenderness

Our threads are entwined, like yarn on a spree,
You knit and I purl—just don't trip on me!
Every stitch tells a tale, goofy and bright,
Of mishaps in dance and our late-night munch bites.

You doodle on napkins, I try to compose,
A song about how you can't find your clothes.
Yet every glance shines like diamonds of fun,
In this tapestry woven by you and by one.

We sketch out our lives with color and cheer,
Mixing laughter with hope as our hearts draw near.
In this fabric of time we wear with delight,
Your goofy expressions make everything right.

So let's keep on laughing beneath this vast sky,
Through patterns of nonsense, we'll soar, you and I.
Each moment a thread that keeps us entwined,
In, oh what a love, whimsically designed!

Celestial Connection

In the cosmos we drift, like two little stars,
You make me feel bright, even in old cars.
With comets of laughter and moons full of glee,
We orbit in rhythm, just you and me.

You stole my heart like a thief in the night,
Leaving behind all my last bites of delight.
Yet each silly moment—like tripping on air,
Makes this cosmic play feel beyond compare.

Let's launch our own rocket, with snacks in a bag,
Captured in time with a giggle and wag.
For every misstep is a star in our dance,
In the universe wild, I'll take every chance.

So here's to our journey through space and through fun,
You make the big bang feel like two hearts as one.
We'll float through the galaxies forevermore,
In the vastness of love, oh, what a score!

www.ingramcontent.com/pod-product-compliance
Lightning Source LLC
Chambersburg PA
CBHW070024020125
19746CB00003B/66

9 789916 948361